The Man in the Gray Suit and Other Short Plays

by Lisa Soland

A SAMUEL FRENCH ACTING EDITION

SAMUEL
FRENCH

FOUNDED 1830

NEW YORK HOLLYWOOD LONDON TORONTO

SAMUELFRENCH.COM

Cover photo courtesy of the Author
Actor: Paul Cuneo

Copyright © 2009 by Lisa Soland

ISBN 978-0-573-69729-6   Printed in U.S.A.   #29164

IMPORTANT BILLING AND CREDIT REQUIREMENTS

INTRODUCTION

I have known Lisa Soland for many many years. I've known her as a friend, a confidant, an actress, a producer, and a playwright. I could go on and on about the first four categories, but it is the fifth, the playwright, that concerns me here.

As a writer myself, I am constantly fascinated by the human condition. My own writing attempts to explore the psychology of normal people in abnormal situations. When telling a story to myself, this is easy. But when trying to write it in a form that others can understand and identify with, ah, there's the problem! Forcing the audience to examine the complexity of the human mind and ego is a difficult task. For one thing, the audience wants to be entertained, not educated. But for the audience to be entertained, they must learn something. I frequently find myself falling over my own words trying to explain complicated issues in a non-complicated manner. Sounds easy? *You* try it.

Lisa Soland is a simple person. And, as a result, frequently angers me.

Of course, that statement needs some explaining, right? No. It's right there, in her work. The simplicity and the reason for my anger.

Lisa's simplicity is how she draws an audience into her work. She doesn't force them or confront them. With subjects as diverse as answering the question "What is the purpose of Art?" or finding the common ground between a couple separated by a huge personal loss, she manages to find a simple and easy way to make those topics, and the characters involved, accessible to the audience.

You see my anger? I'm a writer. I struggle with this every day. She makes it look so darn easy! My only joy is that I happen to know that *she* struggles with it as well. But why does she have to be so good at it?

The simple fact is that she is. Her simplest works have more layers and meanings that the vast majority of complicated works being shown in major houses. Her characters are easily identifiable to the audience. The situations she sets up are recognizable even when foreign to most people's experiences. The methods she uses to manipulate the audience's feelings are crafted so carefully the audience will certainly deny that any such manipulation took place!

And, most upsetting of all to a fellow writer, she makes her audience *think!*

Thank goodness she's also a friend or I'd have nothing to do with her. I certainly wouldn't spend hours over coffee discussing her latest concept or marveling over her casual observations on people who walk by. But I have. And I'm a better writer for it. You can't deal with Lisa or her work without learning something about yourself as well.

However, there is a dark side to Lisa and her work. As easy as she makes it for the audience to be involved, she makes it a challenge for the performers. If you are looking at this book as a possible source of performance material, you are in for some work. As a performer, producer and director, Lisa doesn't cut any slack to the actors and directors. To be honest, her work is demanding. Be prepared to sweat, curse and spend many frustrated nights staying awake, searching for that extra level you just know she's put there. Yes, hard work. But it's the kind of hard work that leads to the intense joy of success.

It is on the basis of my anger that I wholeheartedly recommend this book and these plays. It is with seething frustration that I must urge you to seek out Lisa's works and study them. It is my unfortunate duty to tell you that you have found material that will move and affect your audience. Yes, I must admit, writing this has been a task.

But it has been my absolute joy to tell you about my friend, Lisa Soland, and her amazing talent. Read on and enjoy.

Steven L. Sears
2009

CONTENTS

THE MAN IN THE GRAY SUIT

THE MAN IN THE GRAY SUIT was first produced by Gerry Athas-Vazquez and the Hermosa Beach Writer's Group in the first annual "8 x 10 x HB" ten-minute play festival, at the Second Story Theater in Hermosa Beach, California, on October 25, 2008. Lisa Soland directed with Vincent Archer as assistant director/stage manager, and the play starred Paul Cuneo as *Man*, Melanie Ewbank as *Woman* and Todd Covert as *Sir*.

CHARACTERS

MAN – Dressed in a gray suit, any age. Has a unique and consistently cheerful attitude. (Note: Actor must be able to maintain a bent-over position throughout the play.)

WOMAN – Businesswoman, any age.

SIR – Businessman, any age.

SETTING

In front of a tall office building.

TIME

Tuesday, 3:30 pm.

COSTUMES & PROPS

Man: Gray suit, gray shirt, gray bow tie and gray shoes.

Woman: Business suit, overcoat, briefcase-type purse, cell phone, energy bar and wrist watch.

Sir: Business suit, overcoat, briefcase.

(SETTING: The area in front of a tall office building. The stage is bare but for a bench or cement block used for sitting.)

(AT RISE: **MAN***, wearing a gray suit, is bent over at the waist, as if he's trying to pick something up from the ground.* **WOMAN** *enters from stage left and crosses by* **MAN***. She is text messaging and deep in thought.)*

MAN. *(clears his throat)* Ha-hum.

WOMAN. Oh, you scared me. I thought you were one of those statues.

MAN. No, no I…

WOMAN. You know, those statues? They've got them around office buildings and they look like real people doing things. You're driving down the road and you spot one out of the corner of your eye and the next thing you know, you've almost slammed into the car in front of you.

MAN. No, I was just bending over to…

WOMAN. There's that one up the street with the old lady and a pot of flowers, and even though I know she's there, every day she catches my eye and I almost get into a very serious accident. I really should take another route.

(beat)

Nothing against the statue, mind you. I like that statue very much.

MAN. No, no flowerpot. Just bending over to pick up this piece of paper.

WOMAN. What piece of paper?

MAN. Well, it was here a minute ago. The wind must have blown it away.

WOMAN. What wind? It's not at all windy.

MAN. Well, it was when I bent over.

WOMAN. It was windy yesterday. How long have you been down there?

MAN. What time is it?

WOMAN. Three-thirty.

MAN. I bent over at four, forty-five.

WOMAN. Four, forty-five, yesterday?

MAN. Yes. That's what the fellow said, "Four, forty-five." So, I've been here a while, I guess.

WOMAN. Twenty-three hours! That's pretty hard to believe. Why wouldn't anyone have helped you in that time?

MAN. Well, I'm figurin' now that everyone's been thinking I'm a statue.

WOMAN. Oh, no. Not in front of *this* building. They're too cheap to buy one of those statues for *this* building. They can't even afford to fix the heat. You have to wear mittens, which makes typing an impossibility.

MAN. *(cheerfully interested)* Oh, is that what you do? Type?

WOMAN. No. My assistant does…

MAN. *(to self)* Assistant.

WOMAN. Why didn't you say something? Get someone to help you? You can't blame society for not helping you if you don't speak up?

MAN. That's true. 'Course I've never blamed society much for anything anyway. I just mind my own business.

WOMAN. Well then, why didn't you say something to some-one?

MAN. I don't enjoy talking, to be honest. In fact, this is the most I've talked in…I don't know how long.

WOMAN. What about your wife?

MAN. No, no. I don't have a wife.

WOMAN. Well, it's no wonder. Wives need to be talked to. If you're not going to talk to a wife, there's really no point in having one.

MAN. I don't suppose.

WOMAN. Women are different in that way. We need communication.

MAN. I suppose you're right.

WOMAN. Well, what can I do? You don't look very comfortable.

MAN. It could be worse. I could be bending over backwards.

(They laugh.)

WOMAN. Good point. Can I help make you comfortable somehow?

MAN. I don't think so, unless you're a back specialist.

WOMAN. What do you mean, like a chiropractor?

MAN. Chiro-what?

WOMAN. Chiropractor.

MAN. Now that's an interesting word, isn't it? Chi-ro-pract...

WOMAN. Chiropractor. It's a person who specializes in the skeleton. You know – making sure that one bone is properly stacked up on the other.

MAN. Oh. And there are people who make a living at that?

WOMAN. You don't get out much, do you?

MAN. I do. I got out yesterday.

WOMAN. Well, it doesn't do you much good if getting out gets you all bent over.

MAN. It does, though. Look at me.

WOMAN. *(Analyzing the situation, she crosses behind him, stage right.)* Let's see.

MAN. *(making an announcement)* This is the last time I get out!

WOMAN. That's silly. Don't say that.

MAN. I mean it.

WOMAN. It's good to get out.

MAN. Not for me.

WOMAN. How 'bout if I just pull you up straight? Would that do it?

MAN. I have no idea.

WOMAN. Well, you certainly can't stay the way you are.

MAN. Why?

WOMAN. Because being bent over is no way to be. What will you do? How will you function? Eat or walk? You must be starving.

(She reaches into her purse for an energy bar.)

MAN. Eat or walk?

WOMAN. Yes, everyone must do those things to…well, to live. To survive.

MAN. Gosh, how have I been doing it?

WOMAN. Surviving?

MAN. Yes.

WOMAN. I don't know but you're beginning to frighten me.

(She puts the bar back into her purse.)

Look, I only have a few more minutes here before my four o'clock and I need some time to prepare, you know, catch up from the three-day weekend. Tell me what to do. Tell me how to help you.

MAN. *(cheerfully)* Why don't you go to your meeting and come back later.

WOMAN. What? No. I'm not going to do that. I'm going to help you, uhhh…What's your name?

MAN. My name?

WOMAN. Yes, your name. Mine is Gloria. How do you do?

(WOMAN shakes MAN's immoveable hand)

I work on the seventh floor. "Seventh heaven." That's what we call it because it's lovely. We have plants, rich mahogany furniture, a fantastic view of the city, just no heat. It's lovely, though, really – when the afternoon sun comes in and warms us up. What's your name?

MAN. Uhhh…

WOMAN. Oh, I get it. You don't want to tell me because you think I might report you for loitering.

MAN. Loitering? Yes, I'm afraid of that – you reporting me. I'm trembling all over. Look at me tremble.

WOMAN. No, you're not. You're not afraid at all. What's going on here?

(She crosses in front, to stage left.)

Is this some kind of a practical joke?

MAN. No, I'm not a joke. People don't laugh at me, for the most part. They know not to. They just walk by.

WOMAN. *(losing patience)* Well, why don't you move out of the way?!

(an idea)

That's it! Don't try to straighten up.

(She crosses to sitting area and sits.)

Just come over here and sit down, without straightening. That way I won't have to worry about you during my meeting. Here, come sit.

MAN. *(trying)* Uhh, sorry. My feet don't seem to want to move. They feel heavy. Leadish.

WOMAN. Leadish?

(She rises and crosses to him, trying to help.)

Well, my legs are strong but not my upper body. I have no upper body strength, so I can't very well move you on my own.

(She tries.)

(SIR enters from stage right and crosses left, whistling.)

Oh, here. Let me ask...

(She crosses to SIR.)

MAN. *(grabbing to stop her)* No. No.

WOMAN. Sir! Sir!

MAN. Don't, Gloria.

(MAN returns to exact original, bent-over position.)

WOMAN. Excuse me, hello.

SIR. *(stopping stage left)* Hi.

WOMAN. Would you mind helping us out, here? This man is stuck in this position and he can't seem to unbend, or stand up or move even.

SIR. Is this some kind of joke?

WOMAN. No. It's not a joke. He really can't move. And I'm asking for help. Your help. I'm thinking the two of us can move him together, off to the side maybe, for the time being. And sit him here.

SIR. (*smiling, shaking his head*) Move it off to the side, huh?

WOMAN. Yes, I think that would be fine. (*asking* MAN) Don't you?

(MAN *says nothing.*)

(*to* MAN) Excuse me? Mister?

SIR. Ma'am. That is a statue. A statue? You know, like up the street – the woman with the flowers? They delivered it yesterday. Personally, I think it's great, but it's hard to believe the managers of this building would spend a dime on this thing when they can't even afford to fix the heat. In my household, we keep decorative pieces in their proper perspective – *nonessentials.*

(*beat*)

My wife keeps buying it, you know – wall stuff. She says she's going to list it on eBay and ends up falling in love with it and keeping it. The walls are covered. Makes her feel good, she says. She says it "*Really talks to her.*"

(WOMAN *reacts.*)

But we've got food on the table and a roof over our heads and *heat.* If we ever have problems financially, the wall stuff goes.

(SIR *crosses stage right.*)

But who am I to complain about this piece.

(*referring to* MAN)

I get to look at it, right? I can't look at heat. I guess there's some kind of pleasure in that – looking at a statue of a man bending over.

WOMAN. Statue?

SIR. But I'd enjoy it a lot more if it were a woman. A woman wearing a dress maybe, but who am I?

WOMAN. Statue?

SIR. Yes. If you'd like to move it out of the way...

(He removes his coat and sets briefcase with coat, off to the side.)

...I'll do my best to oblige.

WOMAN. Statue.

SIR. Yes.

WOMAN. *(to MAN)* Mister?

SIR. Ma'am, statues don't...

WOMAN. Talk. Yes, I know that. I know that.

(Becoming lost in thought, she crosses to sitting area and sits.)

SIR. Ma'am?

WOMAN. Oh, sorry.

(She stands.)

I'm fine, thank you. I've been overwrought, really. Overwrought.

MAN. After a three-day weekend?

WOMAN. Did you hear that?

SIR. *(putting on coat and picking up briefcase)* Pardon?

WOMAN. Never mind. Thank you. Sorry to bother you.

SIR. No problem. Good day, then.

WOMAN. Yes. Good day.

(SIR crosses left and exits, whistling.)

Okay. This is like that rabbit thing, right? You're like that rabbit and I'm Jimmy Stewart.

MAN. I have no idea what you're talking about.

WOMAN. But in the end, the rabbit ends up being real. In the end, it's the art that's real.

MAN. ART!!! Thank you. Yes, that's my name. That's what the man said after he said, "Four, forty-five." He said, "We'll place Art here then." And that was that.

WOMAN. Talking art.

MAN. Yes, but I really try not to. Only sometimes.

(He turns towards her.)

To some.

WOMAN. So I see.

(beat)

And what, may I ask, is your purpose?

MAN. Purpose?

WOMAN. Yes, I've always wondered. Now that I've got you here, *talking*, I'd like to ask you what your purpose is, Art.

MAN. I don't know. I dropped a piece of paper and was bending to pick it up.

WOMAN. *(laughing)* Yes, I know.

(suddenly serious)

Bending? So that's it? Bending is your purpose?

MAN. I really think you're trying to make too much of it. Don't think so much.

WOMAN. Now you're trying to get me to *not* think.

MAN. That would be nice, wouldn't it?

WOMAN. Not to think? I thought it was the other way around.

MAN. For some, yes. But not me. Not now. I mean, really. What would you rather do, Gloria? Rest by thinking or rest by *not* thinking?

WOMAN. To be perfectly honest, I'd like to *not* think.

MAN. Exactly.

WOMAN. *(light bulb)* Oh.

(beat)

Thank you. Thank you. I really appreciate that.

(She gathers her things and crosses to exit stage right.)

MAN. Any time.

WOMAN. Thank you.

(She returns to his side and mock-clandestinely whispers.)

Will you be here…later? Tomorrow?

MAN. *(whispering)* Yes, I think so. But it might change.

WOMAN. What?

MAN. My purpose.

WOMAN. *(realizing)* Yes. Yes, of course. Thank you. Bye. Bye, Art.

(She exits off stage right.)

MAN. Bye.

(returning to his exact original, bent-over position)

Bye, Gloria.

(black out)

End of Play

DIFFERENT

DIFFERENT was first produced in March of 2005 as part of The Best of the Rest Fest at The Actors' Theatre in Santa Cruz, California, and was a finalist for the 2005 Kernodle New Play Competition from the University of Arkansas in Fayetteville, Arkansas.

CHARACTERS

SUSAN – A woman in her early twenties.
CHRIS – A woman in her early twenties.

SCENE

A small warm up area in a gym.

TIME

Now.

(SETTING: A small, warm up area in a gym. Perhaps there are some free weights scattered about and a floor mat or two.)

*(AT RISE: **CHRIS** is alone, stretching.)*

SUSAN. *(entering and seeing **CHRIS** alone)* Can I ask you something?

CHRIS. Okay.

SUSAN. Why don't you like me?

CHRIS. Why do you ask?

SUSAN. Some days you come in here and you almost, sort of, talk to me, but I can tell you don't want to and then other days you do your best to avoid me altogether. And since I seem to be here a lot of the times you come in, I'd kinda like to know why, so I don't have to feel this weird feeling every time I see you.

CHRIS. That's why you want to know, so *you* don't have to feel this weird feeling every time you see me?

SUSAN. That's right.

CHRIS. Why don't you just make up your mind not to worry about it?

SUSAN. Because it bothers me that you don't like me. It bothers me.

CHRIS. There are plenty of other people here who do. Why don't you just put your focus on them?

SUSAN. Why don't you want to tell me why?

CHRIS. Because that's not a fun game for me.

SUSAN. What do you mean?

CHRIS. *(taking a breath)* What usually happens when I try to explain to someone why I don't like him or her is that they get defensive. They try to explain to me how I have misread them so. And then I have to sit there

27

and do my best to look like I'm listening. To look like I'm listening to them tell me how wrong I am. It's not fun. I hate listening to people defend themselves.

SUSAN. Maybe they're just trying to explain to you another point of view.

CHRIS. Yes, I guess you could say that. *I* wouldn't say it that way, but I guess *you* could.

SUSAN. What did I do? Just tell me what I did?

CHRIS. You know, sometimes people just don't like each other. There doesn't have to be a reason. There are plenty of people I don't like for no real reason other than we're...different from each other. And there's nothing wrong with that, right? Being different?

SUSAN. One wouldn't think so.

CHRIS. Let's just leave it at that.

SUSAN. Well, if you don't want to tell me why you don't like me, I'm certainly not going to twist your arm.

(pause)

I've noticed that you've gotten really tight in through here. Have you been working on your stomach area or...? Because you look slimmer. You look great. Really great.

(no reply)

Were you *trying* to lose weight or...?

CHRIS. What are you doing?

SUSAN. I'm asking you a question.

CHRIS. Leave me alone.

SUSAN. You're a bitch.

CHRIS. Now comes the name-calling.

SUSAN. You deserve it.

CHRIS. No, I don't. I have a right to not like you. I'm honest. You asked me and I told you. Why does that make me a bitch?

SUSAN. You don't even want to try to be friends.

CHRIS. That's right. I'll be friendly to you, but not friends.

SUSAN. "Friendly?"

CHRIS. Yes, friendly. That means we nod to each other. We smile. And when we have to, we exchange pleasantries about the weather – friendly.

SUSAN. But not friends.

CHRIS. That's right.

SUSAN. Why?

CHRIS. What is up with you today?

SUSAN. I'm just curious.

CHRIS. Number one, as I've been trying to explain, I don't like you. Number two, I have enough friends.

SUSAN. Enough friends? Is that possible – to have enough friends?

CHRIS. For me it is, yes.

SUSAN. Whatever happened to that saying by Walter Brennan, "I've never met a man I didn't like."

CHRIS. Will Rogers.

SUSAN. What?

CHRIS. Nothing.

SUSAN. One should never have enough friends.

CHRIS. Why does that make you uncomfortable, that I have enough?

SUSAN. It doesn't make me uncomfortable.

CHRIS. And because of a few catchy sayings by famous people, suddenly you have to live up to them and over-extend yourself.

SUSAN. They're good sayings and they offer much value to my life.

CHRIS. Good, I'm happy for you.

SUSAN. You must be a very unhappy person.

CHRIS. Personal attacks. Let me look at my watch here. Four minutes into the answering of the question comes the personal attacks. Usually they come before the name-calling. You seem to be out of order.

SUSAN. Listen, I'm just saying that you probably live a lonely life having that attitude about friends. I had a party Saturday night and there were so many people there that the neighbors called the cops. Not 'cause we were causing trouble or anything. It was just because there were so many people packed onto the front lawn that they started to pour out into the street, so some asshole called the cops.

(beat)

If you and I got along a little better than we do, I would have invited you too. We've got a pool and a Jacuzzi. You could have met someone there.

CHRIS. In the Jacuzzi?

SUSAN. Sure. I noticed you work out alone.

CHRIS. God, I'm so glad I studied this sort of thing. Had I run up against you a couple years ago, you could have really screwed with my head.

SUSAN. Okay. I get it. There's nothing I can do. You are just immoveable. I guess there are some people who aren't going to like you, no matter what you do. I guess we just have to leave it at that.

CHRIS. Great.

SUSAN. Have a good workout.

CHRIS. Nice weather we're having.

SUSAN. Fuck you.

CHRIS. No thanks, you're not my type.

SUSAN. Oh, that's it. You're gay! Ah! I should have guessed that from the beginning. You're gay.

CHRIS. You know, I'm actually surprised that it took you 'til now to try that one. You're not as good as I thought.

SUSAN. *(Ignoring her, she continues to press.)* What is it you like about women?

CHRIS. Well, the women I like have restraint. Do you know what that is?

SUSAN. Yes, self-control.

CHRIS. Yes, that's right – self-control.

SUSAN. *(enticingly)* I had an...experience once, with a woman.

CHRIS. *(rises to exit)* Excuse me.

SUSAN. Wait. What? What did I do? Please wait. Chris, right? You're name's Chris. Please. Just sit and talk to me. Please.

(genuinely, or as genuine as possible)

How is someone like me ever going to grow, if someone like you doesn't help?

*(**CHRIS** stops.)*

Please. Just talk to me.

CHRIS. *(correcting **SUSAN**)* With you.

SUSAN. *With* me. Whatever. Don't go. No one like you ever talks to me.

CHRIS. "Like me?" What do you mean, "like me"?

SUSAN. You're...I don't know. Strong.

CHRIS. Strong?

SUSAN. Yeah, strong. And smart. You seem to know a bunch of things I don't. About stuff like...types of people and things. Smart. I'll bet you never let anyone hurt you.

CHRIS. *(an aside, from a calloused, hurting heart)* Well, I don't know about that.

SUSAN. And I know I'm a..."type of person," but God, how am I ever going to change? How do I stand a chance to grow and learn about things if people like you don't try to help me?

CHRIS. *(A chord of compassion has been struck. She returns.)* Okay. What do you want?

SUSAN. I want to know what it is about me you don't like.

CHRIS. *(nice and gentle)* Are you familiar with the word narcissist?

SUSAN. Narcissist. I've heard of it, yes. It's like...to be in love with yourself.

CHRIS. Yes, pretty much.

SUSAN. What does that have to do with me?

CHRIS. Well, let's not get too far ahead of ourselves, now.

(Gently, she continues.)

The word narcissist comes from Narcissus who was this Greek kid who basically falls in love with his reflection in a pool.

SUSAN. *(suddenly remembering something very important)* Oh, that reminds me. Hold on one second. I've got to make one quick call to our...

(She dials her cell phone.)

Hold on. Just a quick...

(into phone)

Johnny! Johnny, listen. There is a gold bracelet at the bottom of the pool.

(beat)

It's mine from Saturday night.

(beat)

When you clean the pool this afternoon, could you just get it out for me? It's worth a ton of money.

(beat)

Oh. Well, can you come back again, later today?

(beat)

Well, it *was* there. I saw it there this morning. Listen, where are you now? Oh, great. Why don't you just swing back over on your way home?

(beat)

Yes, it's important. Okay, great. It's in the deep end.

CHRIS. *(to self)* The deep end.

SUSAN. *(into phone)* Great. Just scoop it out and leave it on the back porch.

(beat)

It's gold, yeah. Leave it on the back porch. Gold! You know, yellow.

CHRIS. *(to self)* Yellow.

SUSAN. Thanks, Johnny. You're a sweetheart.

(She hangs up. To **CHRIS***)*

Now where were we?

CHRIS. You do know, don't you, that Johnny is going to steal your gold bracelet?

SUSAN. See? It's things like that. You know things about types of people and I want you to teach me. I mean, I don't believe you about Johnny because he's not only my pool man...

(whispering)

I've been seeing him.

CHRIS. Screwing him.

SUSAN. What?

CHRIS. Screwing him, right?

SUSAN. I don't know how to take you...to laugh or to be offended.

CHRIS. You want to know what I think?

SUSAN. *(after a brief moment of thinking)* Yes, I do.

CHRIS. You better beat him to your house if you want that bracelet. Because if you don't get there in time, he'll say that he looked for it but couldn't find it. And if you stop to think about it, there's probably been other things missing from around the house, right?

(beat)

SUSAN. Okay, okay. I'm going. One thing at a time.

(turns to go)

I've got to clock out first. I'll talk with you later, Chris. 'Kay?

(beat)

'Kay?

CHRIS. Sure. Sure. Later.

*(***SUSAN*** exits.)*

(**CHRIS** *takes her cell phone out of her purse and dials.*)

Hey, Johnny. We still on for lunch?

(pause as she listens to the excuse)

Oh, I see. No, no, I understand. "When it comes to pools, Johnny's no fool." Not a problem. Business comes first.

(beat)

Sure, that sounds fine.

(beat)

Hey, will you do me a favor? Leave her gold bracelet on the back porch, Johnny. Just like she said. Leave it there.

(blackout)

End of Play

RED ROSES

RED ROSES was first produced on July 21, 2005 in 13th Street Rep Company's New Short Play Festival in New York City, and on September 30, 2005 in Appetite Theatre's Bruschetta 2005: Evening of New Short Plays in Chicago, Illinois.

CHARACTERS

JULIE – A forty year-old writer, carried away with her success. Smart, both in mind and dress. Married to Robert.

ROBERT – Julie's forty-five year-old husband who has become, out of necessity, a work-at-home father. Solid and clear, the stable one.

SETTING

The living room of a married couple with two children.

TIME

Evening, Julie's birthday.

(SETTING: The living room of Robert and Julie's home. Photos of the family with the two children are placed visibly to audience. There are the basics and then some – a couch, chairs and a coffee table, along with JULIE's writing desk.)

(AT RISE: ROBERT is offstage, in the kitchen doing dishes. There is a knock at the door.)

ROBERT. *(Entering from kitchen, he crosses to front door.)* Coming.

(He exits off right.)

Thank you.

(He enters carrying a dozen roses, tastefully arranged in a crystal glass vase and calls over his shoulder, back towards the front door.)

Who are they from...?

(Realizing the deliveryman has left, he sets them on Julie's desk. To self.)

Red roses.

(Crosses upstage and stops at kitchen entrance. Turns back to once again look at roses, then exits into kitchen. A moment. He reappears with towel, drying a bowl and once again contemplates the roses. Exits into kitchen. Another moment. Suddenly, ROBERT re-enters, strides to desk, swipes card out of plastic fork and holds it up to the light. Embarrassed at himself.)

What am I doing?!

(Puts card back into arrangement and exits into bedroom. Re-enters with a small book. Reading aloud.)

"Blooming Implications: The Hidden Meaning of Flowers."

(He searches frantically through the pages.)

ROBERT. *(cont.)* Roses. Roses.

(finding it)

"Roses!" Got it. Okay...

(turning pages)

Pink...yellow... white...red.

(finding it)

"Red!"

(reading from book)

"Roses are an exquisite expression of love, all types of love, but the red rose is the ultimate in completing the tender passion. Usually sent following a night of untamed lovemaking..."

*(**ROBERT** slams book down on coffee table and retrieves card from flower arrangement. He moves to where there is stronger light so he can study it without having to open it. Just then we hear **JULIE**.)*

JULIE. *(from offstage)* Hello. I'm back.

ROBERT. *(rushing to replace card in its original position)* Hey. How was your trip?

JULIE. *(She opens door with keys and enters with suitcase and purse. Leaving the suitcase at the door, she crosses to mirror on wall.)* Great. I'm exhausted. My feet are killing me.

(checks herself out in mirror)

Where are the kids?

ROBERT. Weren't you due in at five?

JULIE. *(still into mirror)* Yes. It's a long story.

*(**JULIE** exits.)*

ROBERT. I'm here.

JULIE. *(from offstage)* Sabastian! Kendall!

(re-entering)

Where are they?

ROBERT. I dropped them off at the Bergh's so we could still make our six o'clock dinner reservation.

JULIE. *(gasping)* Oh my God. I'm so sorry. I can't believe I did that. Where is my brain?

ROBERT. *(under his breath)* It's not your brain I'm worried about.

JULIE. Can we quick change the reservation? Where is it?

ROBERT. Gladstone's on Easter? I don't think so.

JULIE. I'm so sorry.

(sits on couch and removes shoes)

ROBERT. *(picking up Julie's suitcase, crosses to bedroom)* Well anyway, the kids are at the Bergh's, your mail is on the desk and…oh, those flowers came for you.

(exits)

JULIE. Flowers?

*(***JULIE*** *rises and crosses to flowers. She reads the card as* **ROBERT** *quietly reappears in doorway.)*

ROBERT. Who are they from?

JULIE. *(startled)* Huh? Oh, I don't know.

ROBERT. You don't know.

JULIE. No. It doesn't say.

ROBERT. That's not the right answer.

JULIE. That's not the right answer?

ROBERT. No.

JULIE. Okay. What is the right answer?

ROBERT. "You, darling." "They're from you, darling," is the right answer.

JULIE. But they're not from you.

ROBERT. How do you know that?

JULIE. It's not your writing.

ROBERT. The people at the flower shop write what you tell them to write. Of course it's not my writing!

JULIE. Okay. So they are from you?

ROBERT. No.

JULIE. Why are you getting so upset?

ROBERT. Because they're not from me. Who are they from, Julie?

JULIE. I don't know, Robert. They could be from a number of different people. It's my fortieth birthday.

ROBERT. What's the card say?

JULIE. What?

ROBERT. What does the card say?

JULIE. This is not like you at all.

ROBERT. "This is not like me at all." "This is not like me at all?!" Guess what else is "not like me at all?" Running this house is "not like me," that's what. Directing traffic at the cross walk. Driving the kids from school to field hockey, to home, to Scottie's, is "not like me at all." I am tired of pancake batter and wiping up their faces and then the floor. And when I finally have a moment to myself, to sand, to work, to do what it is I am put on this earth to do, which I should be doing at the studio...

(corrects himself)

Workshop.

(continuing, even more angry)

...the doorbell rings and it's the "completion of the tender passion." Now, what does the card say, Julie?

JULIE. *(reading)* "Happy birthday, Sweetheart."

ROBERT. "Happy birthday, Sweetheart." Oh. Okay. And you don't know who they're from?

JULIE. *(staring at* **ROBERT***)* I've never seen you like this before.

ROBERT. And you don't know who they're from?!

JULIE. No.

ROBERT. *(Beat. Retrieves cordless phone.)* Ya know what? I'm going to call that publisher-guy-friend of yours and have a little chat. What's his name?

JULIE. What are you talking about?

ROBERT. What's his name?

JULIE. Which one? I work with seven different...

ROBERT. You know which one – the guy with the oiled hair, and the suspenders with the matching socks. The one who for some strange reason, volunteers to take you to the airport every time you need to go anywhere because you've got to sign books on the way. That "which one."

JULIE. I think the name you want is Darryl.

ROBERT. "Darryl!" What's the number?

JULIE. 310-578-2900.

(**ROBERT** *dials as she dictates from memory.*)

ROBERT. (*looking at watch*) He'd never be back to the office this quickly.

(*hangs up the phone*)

JULIE. That's the home number.

ROBERT. (*pause*) Uh-hah.

JULIE. It's not what you think.

ROBERT. Okay.

(**ROBERT** *exits into bedroom. After a moment he re-enters with an arm full of pressed jeans, shirts on hangers and a canvas overnight bag. He sets all items on couch and begins to pack.*)

JULIE. What are you doing?

ROBERT. Not what *you* think.

JULIE. (*picking up phone from coffee table*) Robert, don't do this! Please. Here's the phone. Just hit the redial.

ROBERT. (*Who has been grappling with well starched and pressed blue jeans on hangers. He holds them out to her.*) I don't want my jeans sent to the cleaners. Okay? I want them thrown into the washer and then the dryer and then folded and put into a regular drawer made out of strong, sturdy wood. I don't care how much money you're making. I never did anything for the money.

There was a time, a very happy time, when we had none. I don't want pleats or this bullshit. Do you hear me?

(handing her the "Blooming Implications" book, left open)

ROBERT. *(cont.)* I've put up with all these stupid little things, these things that somehow make you feel as though you're successful in life because I had the most important thing of all – you. I had you. Now that that's not mine anymore, don't...

JULIE. I am yours. Believe me!

ROBERT. Now that that's not mine anymore, DON'T PRESS MY JEANS!!!

(jams clothes into canvas bag, exits front door)

JULIE. *(The book open in her hand, she reads aloud.)* "The tender passion...?"

(crosses to the front door and calls after him)

You know, people who believe everything they read, shouldn't read.

(She re-enters, sits on couch.)

ROBERT. *(after a moment, re-entering)* And people who write books shouldn't lie. Have you been lying to me, Julie?

JULIE. Robert, listen to me. I am very happy. I'm still in love with you after fifteen years and...

ROBERT. *(quietly)* You're still in love with me?

(sarcastically)

Well, thank God for that.

JULIE. ...and yes, we're successful and we have money when I used to worry about paying rent. I don't think that's a bad thing.

ROBERT. I want you to look me straight in the eyes and tell me that you did not sleep with this guy.

JULIE. I'm in love with you.

ROBERT. Look me right in the eye and tell me.

JULIE. Robert, you're everything to me.

ROBERT. Tell me!

    (JULIE lowers her head.)

What did I do? Could you please tell me what I could have possibly done?

    (JULIE says nothing.)

I always thought that if I opened myself up... If I was more sensitive, more understanding... But it isn't enough. Love isn't enough.

JULIE. Why don't we...?

ROBERT. No. You do not get to make this decision.

JULIE. I was just going to...

ROBERT. No!

    (beat)

I'm trying to decide if I want to hear the details and I can't think with you trying to change the direction on me. Let me think.

JULIE. *(carefully)* I was just going to say that maybe we should look into getting some counseling.

ROBERT. Counseling?! For what?! We don't need counseling. Counseling is for when there's a communication problem. We don't have a communication problem. You do. This is your problem. I don't need to go and pay some complete stranger to tell me that you have a communication problem. If you were unhappy...

JULIE. I am not unhappy.

ROBERT. ...you should have told me. We would have...

JULIE. I'm not unhappy.

ROBERT. ...worked it out.

    (pointing to roses)

Then what is this? Could you tell me that?

JULIE. I don't know. I've just been very busy and...

ROBERT. ...and Darryl was there.

JULIE. *(no response)*

ROBERT. What do you want me to do? Travel with you?

(JULIE *shakes her head.*)

Because there's going to be another Darryl, you know. There's always another Darryl waiting in the lining of your books and you know what? They're not bad people. They're just lonely and empty inside, and somehow when the feelings line up, there the two of you are.

(JULIE *rises, crosses stage left.*)

The question is – what do you want? For good. Is it this dishonesty? Or is it a higher thing?

(*beat*)

Something inhuman, actually, now that I think of it. These are the things you need to think about.

JULIE. (*looking at him*) I don't need to think...

ROBERT. Yes, actually you do because I'd like for you to stay home. I don't want you to tour anymore.

JULIE. (*concerned*) Robert, I can't do that...

ROBERT. You can write your books here, with us, like you used to. And then when you have to tour, have your publishers plan one that fits into our schedule – not theirs.

JULIE. I don't know if I have that kind of weight yet.

ROBERT. Well, now's the time to find out because if you don't...I'm not up for it. That's your choice.

JULIE. (*beat*) I'll do whatever you tell me.

ROBERT. Okay.

(*He gets the phone and hands it to her.*)

Redial.

JULIE. (*hits the redial button and sits in chair next to couch*) Answering machine.

(**ROBERT** *sits on couch and nods to leave message.*)

(*into phone*)

Yes, Darryl? This is Julie. When you get in give me a call...

(beat)

JULIE. *(cont.)* Oh, Darryl? Hi. Yes, everything's fine. Listen, I got the flowers. Well, they came to the house, here.

(beat)

It's Easter. The office is closed.

(beat)

Uh-hah. Uh-hah.

(beat)

Well listen, there's something I…

ROBERT. *(taking the phone from her, then coolly, without a breath)* Darryl, this is Julie's husband. We've been talking this evening and we've decided that it's over.

(beat)

She's not going to be finishing this particular tour so you've got yourself some calls to make. And next time around, if she decides to go with your publishing company, the two of us will meet with some *other* member of your "staff" to discuss only the priority cities. Are you going to have a problem with this?

(pause)

Terrific. Happy Easter.

(ROBERT hangs up the phone and turns to JULIE. A moment.)

JULIE. I'm sorry.

(ROBERT continues to stare at her then exits into the kitchen. JULIE rises, crosses to front door, picks up Robert's luggage, and carries it to couch. She opens it and starts to unpack his jeans.)

ROBERT. *(Entering quietly, he crosses to JULIE.)* What are you doing?

JULIE. I'm going to take these jeans…

(fighting tears)

JULIE. (*cont.*)...and I'm going to throw them into the washer, and then the dryer, and then I'm going to fold them and place them in a drawer made out of strong, study wood.

(*extends arm, offering pair of jeans*)

Do you want to help?

(*silence*)

(**ROBERT** *stares at jeans then slowly takes the pair from her.* **JULIE** *picks up a second pair and together they twist and pull at them, trying to rid them of their pressed seems, as the lights slowly fade*)

End of Play

THE SAME THING

THE SAME THING was first produced on February 3, by TeCo Theatrical Productions, Inc. as part of their 2005 New Play Competition in Dallas, Texas. Lisa Soland directed the play, Rachel Lamb choreographed, Carter Hudson played *Man* and Danni Wilkins played *Woman.*

CHARACTERS

WOMAN – A woman, any age.
MAN – A man, any age.

SETTING

The aisle of a grocery store.

TIME

Now.

(SETTING: The aisle of a grocery store.)

*(AT RISE: **MAN** enters stage left and **WOMAN** stage right, pushing shopping carts partially filled with food and beverages. She is shopping facing downstage and he is shopping facing upstage. As they come near to each other, instead of one going one way and the other going the other way, they run into each other. In hopes to remedy the situation, they each move to get out of the way, once again...running into each other. Believe it or not, they do this one more time and then begin to laugh.)*

WOMAN. *(laughing)* Care for a dance?

(Continuing to laugh, they both get out of the way and begin to cross by each other and away.)

MAN. I'm so sorry.

WOMAN. It's my fault, really.

MAN. Oh, I'd hardly say it was your fault. We both just seem to be thinking along the same lines.

WOMAN. Yes, we are aren't we?

MAN. Yes, it's interesting.

WOMAN. How so?

MAN. Well...never mind.

(He continues to exit stage right.)

WOMAN. No, really. I'd like to hear.

MAN. *(He stops to explain.)* Well, if one of us were not as kind, more rude I should say, we wouldn't be having this problem at all.

WOMAN. We're running into each other because we're kind?

MAN. Yes. See, we're courteous people. We are of the like that try to accommodate the environmental space of another.

WOMAN. *(nodding)* Yes, I see what you're saying.

MAN. Therefore, we both try at the same time to move out of the way, resulting only in…

WOMAN. …getting back into the way of the other.

MAN. Yes. Very exciting, actually.

WOMAN. Exciting?

MAN. Oh, yes. You see, in all my past relationships, I've always been "the adjustor," the one who gets out of the way, the one who apologizes when it's needed so that the relationship can continue. I've never really had the thought to actively pursue one who is more like me – kind.

WOMAN. That *is* interesting. I have a similar background. My past relationships have been nothing but struggle. Trying hard, very hard to please and then waking up one day and realizing that I'm the only one who's trying. "The lone and selfless giver." That's me.

MAN. You got it, exactly. This is quite amazing. I've never really run into another…me.

WOMAN. Well, I'm sure we're different in other ways.

MAN. Really? You think so?

WOMAN. Oh, we must be. Everyone's different, aren't they?

MAN. Well, let's see.

(*He turns his shopping cart around and faces her.*)

Do you like to tango?

WOMAN. Actually, I do. I happen to love it. I've studied since I was five.

MAN. Five?

WOMAN. Yes.

MAN. Me too.

WOMAN. No kidding.

MAN. Five. I kid you not. I love it passionately.

WOMAN. Oh, that's just a coincidence. Remarkable, at that.

MAN. Yes, I'd say so.

WOMAN. *(She turns her cart around and faces him.)* How many brothers and sisters do you have?

MAN. Three.

WOMAN. Me too.

MAN. Two brothers and one sister.

WOMAN. Me too, exactly. Where do you fall?

MAN. I'm third.

WOMAN. Me too.

MAN. Third?

WOMAN. Yes.

MAN. Remarkable.

WOMAN. This is getting quite hard to believe.

MAN. Oh, I don't know. It was bound to happen at some point. You spend a lifetime running into people who are different from you...

WOMAN. Very different.

MAN. Yes.

WOMAN. *(with some pain)* Different and difficult.

MAN. Yes, very different and then suddenly one day, presto – a match.

WOMAN. *(tentatively)* Well, I don't know if I'd say we were a match.

MAN. *(recognizing her tentativeness)* Oh, very sorry. I was not insinuating that we...the two of us...

WOMAN. ...get together?

MAN. No, not at all. I'm single but I would never presume that you were.

WOMAN. I am, actually.

MAN. Single?

WOMAN. Yes.

> *(beat)*

> Very.

MAN. What do you know about that?

WOMAN. But still...

MAN. Oh, yes. But still we can't just assume that we, the two of us, would ever…go out.

WOMAN. Well, if we did…go out…

MAN. Yes?

WOMAN. If we did, I'm sure we would find, through continued conversation, many areas where we differ.

MAN. Of course, it's natural.

WOMAN. What we're experiencing now, is *not* natural.

MAN. Not based on my experience.

WOMAN. *(She steps towards him quickly and asks…)* Do you go to church?

MAN. *(stepping towards her quickly)* Every Sunday.

WOMAN. You're kidding? I thought for sure I'd get you there.

MAN. Nope, every Sunday.

(quickly turning out to audience)

Early service?

WOMAN. *(turns out as well)* Every time. Starts the day out right.

MAN. You are a woman after my own heart.

WOMAN. You know, this is remarkable. To be quite honest, I've always wanted to marry a man who already went to church, you know?

MAN. Yes. So you wouldn't have to talk him into it.

WOMAN. Exactly. I tried that.

MAN. Didn't work, huh?

WOMAN. Well, it does, you know. For a while. Then when they've got you, here…

(She points to her heart.)

…in the heart…it fades. It all fades.

MAN. *(nodding)* Yes. I've dated many fading women.

WOMAN. I guess the trick is to marry someone you like as they are, right from the start.

MAN. Yes, the problem is finding someone you like.

WOMAN. Yes.

MAN. I suppose it would be narcissistic of us if we were to... go out.

WOMAN. Narcissistic? Why?

MAN. Well, it would be like dating ourselves. Like the ol' clown falling in love with his reflection. I'm sure it would fail, eventually. We would have nothing to talk about.

WOMAN. We don't seem to be having a problem yet.

MAN. Yes, that's true. But still, I suppose one needs conflict in their lives, for...

(trying to think)

...something, right?

WOMAN. Conflict?

MAN. Yes, you know. To keep you on your toes.

(He stands on his toes to demonstrate.)

WOMAN. I'm tired of being on my toes. I'd actually like to be able to stand using all parts of my feet.

MAN. Yes. That does sound appealing, doesn't it?

(They share a moment of depth and intimacy which he breaks by glancing into her shopping cart.)

Oh, I see you like frozen dinners as well.

(He takes one of his "Hungry Man" frozen dinners out of his cart.)

WOMAN. Well, I don't actually *like* them.

(She takes one of her "Healthy Choice" frozen dinners out of her cart.)

I buy them because I don't like to cook.

MAN. *(Excited, he steps towards her.)* Oh, you don't like to cook? I love to cook.

WOMAN. *(clarifying)* Well...I don't like to cook for just me.

MAN. Yes, it's horrible. That's why I buy the testy things.

(He tosses his dinner back into his cart.)

WOMAN. Yes, they're great. Just pop them into the oven and VOILÁ.

MAN. Yes, very convenient.

(quickly)

Do you like to give or receive?

WOMAN. Pardon?

MAN. *(more gently)* Do you like to give or receive?

WOMAN. *(It occurs to her what he's saying and is embarrassed.)* Oh…my.

MAN. I'm sorry to embarrass you but I've got to know, it's killing me.

WOMAN. Oh.

MAN. Actually, I probably already know the answer – give, right?

WOMAN. *(sweetly)* Well…yes.

MAN. Me too. And there lies our healthy conflict.

WOMAN. Excuse me?

MAN. Our healthy conflict. We would both have to learn to receive. Look…

(beat)

What's your name?

WOMAN. Jean.

MAN. Jean?! No way!! No WAY!!!

WOMAN. Yes, my name is Jean.

MAN. *My* name is Gene.

WOMAN. Oh, my God.

MAN. I can't believe it. This is the twilight zone, right here and now.

WOMAN. I feel like I'm dreaming.

MAN. Man, if this is a dream, let us sleep on! This is remarkable. The most remarkable day of my life!!!

WOMAN. *(trying to remain composed)* Well, now. Let's keep our heads. You were saying?

MAN. *(due to her hesitancy, also trying to remain composed)* Yes, Jean…not that you and I are going to…

WOMAN. Date.

MAN. Date, yes. I don't want to presume that we would conclude this conversation in dating, but if we were...

WOMAN. If.

MAN. If we were...to go out...

(They both move slowly towards each other during the next few lines.)

...since we are by nature, givers, we would have to then learn to receive.

(They move closer.)

WOMAN. Therefore, living a much more balanced...

MAN. ...and fulfilling...

(closer)

WOMAN. Existence.

MAN. Exactly.

(They go to...maybe kiss, then she pulls away.)

WOMAN. It's too much really.

MAN. Too much?

WOMAN. Yes. It's almost too much to handle.

(She hides behind her cart and without conscious awareness, steps up onto the back bar.)

We're finishing each other's sentences!

MAN. *(Growing nervous, he crosses to the front of her cart.)* So, what are you saying?

(When she answers, he listens so intently, that without knowing it, he pushes her around, upstage, in half a circle during the next few lines.)

WOMAN. I'm not used to this...this functioning communication and it's hard for me.

MAN. If being happy and fulfilled is hard for you...

WOMAN. If you only knew what I've been through...

MAN. ...and it would be cause for you to walk away...

WOMAN. ...the experiences I've had over and over and over again.

MAN. ...then there's where we differ.

WOMAN. We differ?

(The cart movement stops.)

MAN. Yes. Because I would never walk away from anything that had a pinch of a promise that by moving forward, I would be more happy. Never.

WOMAN. Yes, that is where we differ.

(She steps down off the cart.)

New things are very hard for me.

MAN. The tango was new for you, at one time.

WOMAN. I was five.

MAN. *(To move closer, he steps up on front of cart.)* You can be five again.

(WOMAN is hesitating so he takes her by the hands and kneels down on one knee in front of her.)

Look, Jean. I would like to date you, to take you out on the town, to wine and dine you with fabulous home-made meals and treat you...well, to give and give and give to you, but I understand completely, if because of fear, you have to say no.

WOMAN. *(moving away)* No.

(beat)

It's not for me, Gene. I'm very sorry.

MAN. *(Sadly defeated, he rises and dusts off pants.)* I understand. It's all right. Well, goodbye, Jean.

(He steps in to shake her hand.)

WOMAN. *(shaking his hand)* Goodbye...Gene.

MAN. *(deeply sincere)* It's been more than a pleasure talking with you.

WOMAN. *(deeply sincere)* Same to you.

(They cross back to their carts and start to go but both

try to go the same way again. They smile kindly, and then both try to get out of each other's way by going in the same direction...again. Believe it or not, it happens a third time and then they stop.)

WOMAN. *(cont.) (Recognizing that this is a sign, she gives in.)* Well, what do you know about that? We're doing the same thing.

MAN. The same thing. What do you know.

(Having already moved on, he tries to exit.)

WOMAN. *(Coyly, she steps in his path, stopping him.)* I don't mind the same thing...Gene.

MAN. *(hopeful)* The same thing is good.

WOMAN. *(She takes a single rose out of her cart.)* Care for a tango?

MAN. *(He pushes his cart out of the way.)* I thought you'd never ask.

(The tango music begins and they quickly snap into the starting position. She puts the rose between her teeth and they begin. She leads and the two dance stage right and then he leads and the two dance stage left. On their way off stage she turns and swoops up her purse and off they go with flair. Music swells.)

(blackout)

End of Play

KNOTS

KNOTS was first produced on October 13, 2006 under the title, *More Than Anything Else in the World*, in The Renaissance Guild's One-Act Series at the Jump Start Theatre, San Antonio's Premiere Black Theatre Company in San Antonio, Texas. The play was directed by Sharon Renee Shepherd and starred Chris Sampayo as *Doug*, Niki Fernandez as *Karen* and Cynthia Castro as *Older Woman*.

CHARACTERS

OLDER WOMAN – A middle-aged woman – Karen, many years later.
KAREN – College student, about 20.
DOUG – College student, about 20.

SETTING

Doug's childhood bedroom in his parent's home in West Palm Beach, Florida.

TIME

Today.

*(**SETTING**: Doug's bedroom, which consists primarily of a twin sized bed.)*

*(**AT RISE**: **DOUG** and **KAREN** are sitting on the bed. **OLDER WOMAN** addresses the audience.)*

OLDER WOMAN. *(to audience)* I dated this guy in college, kind of a co-dependant type, you know – always telling you he loved you. But he had a car, which was great, 'cause we got to go places. One time, we were visiting his folks in West Palm during spring break and we're in his bedroom from when he was a kid, sitting on the bed, and he tells me…

DOUG. *(to **KAREN**)* I love you more than anything else in the world.

OLDER WOMAN. And I'm thinkin', "Crap. I hope he doesn't expect me to tell him that back because…I don't. In fact, I can think of a ton of things I love better than him…like *me*, for instance." Anyway, he says it, just the same.

DOUG. *(to **KAREN**, repeating just as before)* I love you more than anything else in the world.

OLDER WOMAN. And I'm sitting there looking at him. Just looking at him. It's a lot of pressure, you know – sitting there in the room he grew up *in*, on the bed he grew up *on*, with his parents and everyone running around the house. So I thought I'd better smile and say… something.

KAREN. *(She smiles.)* Oh, that's so nice to say. Wow, thanks honey. Thank you. Thanks a lot.

(She pats his hand.)

OLDER WOMAN. And then it comes. The guilt trip. Subtle at first and then the ol' freakin' guilt trip.

DOUG. What? Don't you feel that way too?

KAREN. What way?

DOUG. What I just said.

KAREN. What?

DOUG. You heard me.

OLDER WOMAN. *(to* **DOUG**, *though he doesn't hear her)* Yes, she did. But it gives her time to think if you repeat yourself. So please, just patiently repeat yourself.

DOUG. *(patiently)* I said that I loved you more than anything else in the world.

OLDER WOMAN. Good boy.

(then turning to **KAREN***)*

Thinking. Thinking.

KAREN. Okay. Okay. And I said, "Thanks." Thanks.

DOUG. You don't feel the same way.

KAREN. Well, I don't think I would word it quite like that.

DOUG. You don't love me.

KAREN. No, no that's not it. I do love you.

DOUG. Then why don't you say it?

(She does.)

KAREN. I love you.

DOUG. No, you don't.

KAREN. Yes, I do. I love you, Doug. I love you.

DOUG. No...

(to himself)

What is it? I'm picking up on something but I can't quite put my finger on it.

KAREN. Put your finger on what?

DOUG. You. I can't put my finger on you.

KAREN. Okay.

DOUG. You may love me but it's not quite the same.

KAREN. Not quite the same as what?

DOUG. As me. As me, Karen. You don't love me like I love you.

KAREN. Okay.

DOUG. Why do you keep saying that – "Okay," like that? What's that supposed to mean?

KAREN. It means okay. That's all. It means okay.

DOUG. *(realizing)* You don't love me like I love you. That's what it is!

KAREN. Well, how exactly do you love me that's so different?

DOUG. I love you more than anything else in the world, Karen. That's how I love you that's so different.

KAREN. But what exactly does that mean?

DOUG. What do you mean, what does it mean? It means what it means. It means there's nothing I love more. I don't love skiing more than you, reading great literature more than you, food, lobster more than you, uhm… All my favorite things. The beach. The sun. Margaritas. Jimmy Buffet. Nothing. Nothing more than you. Not my parents, not my brother, not my dog. Nothing. You are it.

KAREN. Not your dog?

DOUG. Nothing more than you.

KAREN. Really?

DOUG. Can you say that, Karen? Can you say that you feel that way about me?

(pause)

KAREN. I don't have a dog.

DOUG. *(He closes his eyes, so angry and so hurt.)* Can you say that about me?

KAREN. No. No, I can't.

DOUG. No! No?!!! Why not?

KAREN. I don't know. I just can't.

DOUG. Well, that's just great. That's just great. Thanks a lot. Thanks a lot, Karen. What am I supposed to do now? What am I supposed to do now, huh?!!!

OLDER WOMAN. Oh, throw a fit. You always did.

KAREN. I don't know.

OLDER WOMAN. Throw a fit until I tie myself into a knot.

DOUG. *(throwing a fit)* I don't understand why you just can't say it. Why can't you just fucking say it, Karen? Is it so hard to say something, anything, even if it's not exactly what you mean? What the hell is your fucking problem, anyway? Did your parents raise you so fucking straight that you can never, ever say anything slightly different than what you really, truly, deeply-in-your-heart mean? Huh?!!! What's wrong with you?!!!

OLDER WOMAN. *(simply)* She can't say it 'cause it ain't true.

KAREN. *(sweetly)* You want me to lie?

DOUG. No, I don't want you to lie.

OLDER WOMAN. He wants you to lie.

DOUG. I want you to feel the same way I do.

OLDER WOMAN. *(to audience)* Saying, "Okay" gave me time to think. That's why I said it – to give myself time to think. It's a great word, – "Okay." It's like talking about the weather but you don't have to talk about the weather you just say "okay" instead. So I said it...

KAREN. Okay.

OLDER WOMAN. ...which gave me a good five seconds more to think.

(beat)

And then he said it.

DOUG. *(Lost, he throws up his arms, sarcastic.)* "Okay."

OLDER WOMAN. And then he added the word...

DOUG. Great.

OLDER WOMAN. ...which bought me another five or six seconds.

(beat)

And in that time I thought, "Jeez, I'm stuck down here in West Palm and there ain't no way I'm getting back up to Tallahassee on my own so I better try to figure out how to get myself out of this...gracefully."

KAREN. *(very convincing)* Listen, Doug. I love you. I love you. Just because I can't say it the same way you can, using the same words you do, doesn't mean that my words mean any less. Love is love. It's love, honey. I love you.

OLDER WOMAN. Oh my God.

*(to **KAREN**)*

You love the fact that he has a car and that you don't have any money and that you don't "love" walking five hundred miles to get back to where you need to be so you can be yourself – alone, free. Remember that? Remember YOURSELF? Remember what that feels like to be honest and free and not have to lie? Not have to change yourself to make something work? Not have to tie yourself up into knots like one of those fattening, salty pretzels you buy at the mall when you've hit middle age? Knots, Karen. Remember knots?

(beat)

Be clear. At least in your own head, please be clear about what it is you love.

*(whispering in **KAREN**'s ear)*

His car. You love his car.

KAREN. *(to **DOUG**, ignoring **OLDER WOMAN**)* I love *you.* Okay.

(taking his hand)

I love you, honey.

DOUG. All right. I'm sorry.

KAREN. It's okay.

OLDER WOMAN. *(nodding)* Knots.

(fade out)

End of Play

COME TO THE GARDEN

COME TO THE GARDEN was first produced on June 5, 2006 by Theatre Limina as part of the Summer Shorts III: Double Vision Festival, Bryan Lake Bowl Theater in Minneapolis, Minnesota. Vision #1 was directed by Steve Moulds, with Megan Lee-Erickson playing *Wife* and Steve Moulds playing *Husband*. Vision #2 was directed by Jody Bee, with Kathy Kupiecki playing *Wife* and Eric Mahutga playing *Husband*.

CHARACTERS

WIFE – Mourning the loss of her third child.

HUSBAND – Husband to Wife, who works hard to support them. Mourning as well, in his own, quiet way.

SETTING

The bedroom of a married couple.

TIME

Early evening.

(SETTING: Wife and Husband's bedroom.)

*(AT RISE: **WIFE** is lying on the bed and **HUSBAND** is standing beside her. She is holding a hand-made baby's blanket.)*

HUSBAND. Come to the garden.

WIFE. No.

HUSBAND. It'll make you feel better.

WIFE. I miss you.

HUSBAND. I'm here.

WIFE. I miss how things were.

HUSBAND. I miss you, too.

WIFE. You do?

HUSBAND. Yes, of course, I do.

WIFE. When? When do you miss me?

HUSBAND. Every moment of every day.

WIFE. Now?

HUSBAND. No.

WIFE. Why?

HUSBAND. Because I have you now, here with me.

WIFE. Oh.

HUSBAND. Come with me.

WIFE. No. Lie down.

HUSBAND. I can't.

WIFE. Why not?

HUSBAND. Because I'll fall asleep and I still have some work to do.

WIFE. Lie down and hold me.

HUSBAND. I'll sit here, okay? I'll sit right here so I can look into your eyes.

WIFE. My eyes? Fine.

(**HUSBAND** *sits.*)

HUSBAND. Did you go outside today?

WIFE. No.

HUSBAND. Did you eat?

WIFE. Eat?

HUSBAND. Yes.

WIFE. No.

HUSBAND. What did you do?

WIFE. You ask me that as if you expect I did nothing.

HUSBAND. No. No, I didn't.

WIFE. I did many things.

HUSBAND. Fine.

WIFE. Many things.

HUSBAND. Fine.

WIFE. You don't notice all the things I do but that doesn't mean I didn't do them.

HUSBAND. I know. That's fine.

WIFE. And I didn't watch TV and I didn't take a nap.

HUSBAND. You must be tired.

WIFE. Lie down with me.

HUSBAND. *(avoiding)* Tell me about your day.

WIFE. There's nothing to tell. Boring. Just boring. I can't figure out what's wrong with me.

HUSBAND. Maybe there's nothing wrong with you.

WIFE. Then why do I keep crying? Crying, crying, crying.

HUSBAND. Well, okay – what's wrong with you then? If you were to guess what's wrong with you, what would it be?

WIFE. Uhm. I don't know.

HUSBAND. Guess.

WIFE. Just guess?

HUSBAND. Yes.

WIFE. I'm tired.

HUSBAND. Why don't you go to bed? Just go to bed early tonight.

WIFE. Eight-o'clock?!

HUSBAND. Sure. When one is tired, they should sleep. When one is hungry, they should eat. And so on and so forth.

WIFE. And so on and so forth. I'm tired all the time. It's a sign of depression. Do you think I'm depressed?

HUSBAND. I guess you could be.

WIFE. Really?

HUSBAND. Sure, why not.

WIFE. I miss you. You leave too early now and you come home too late. I miss us lying together in the morning. Come lie with me.

HUSBAND. Oh…

WIFE. Come on.

HUSBAND. Let's go out to the garden. Remember the garden?

WIFE. No.

HUSBAND. Did you work in the garden today?

WIFE. No. I said I didn't go out.

HUSBAND. Right.

WIFE. You don't really listen either. When I'm talking I can tell you're mind is a thousand miles away.

   (beat)

   Where is your mind right now? What are you thinking about?

HUSBAND. Your eyes and the garden.

WIFE. *(impatiently)* The garden, the garden.

HUSBAND. Why don't you work in it anymore?

WIFE. I'm tired of looking at it.

HUSBAND. It used to bring you such joy.

WIFE. It tires me.

HUSBAND. Everything tires you. That doesn't mean there's something wrong with the garden.

WIFE. Lie down with me.

HUSBAND. Come to the garden.

WIFE. No!!! That garden never produces anything. Nothing at all. I work. I slave. And the corn gets knee high by the fourth of July and then it dies. What in the hell is that about? And the tomatoes. So large. So pregnant with promise and then, just before we're to pick them, just before the red is almost perfectly ripe, some deviant, evil thing starts tearing away at it. Small bites at first and the next thing you know it's crawling with something or other and we've lost it. We've lost it.

(She begins to cry.)

All that promise just flushed down the toilet. Flushed down the toilet before it's even got a name. Before we even have time to name it, it's gone. I'm done with it, Honey. I'm done. Three is too many to lose. I'm done.

HUSBAND. I know.

WIFE. I'm not stepping foot in that fucking garden ever again.

HUSBAND. Okay.

WIFE. Never.

HUSBAND. Okay.

(beat)

Why don't you rest? The doctor said you need to rest.

WIFE. Lie down with me.

HUSBAND. Okay. Move over.

(WIFE gladly moves over.)

Are you my love?

WIFE. *(calming down some)* Yes. I love you.

HUSBAND. I love you too.

WIFE. I love when you lie with me.

HUSBAND. I love it too.

(pause)

WIFE. I remember when I was a little girl. I used to plant the garden with my uncle Cal. He taught me how to plant. He taught me about corn – twenty hills per row, seven seeds per hill. We'd do a long row, one hill at a time, carefully laying the seeds into the dirt. He'd prepare the dirt and I'd lay the seed. Once I remember I took a big handful of seeds and worked my way down the row, laying them as I went, all the way to the end and finished with no seeds. I ended perfectly, using every seed I had in my hands and had none left over. Isn't that amazing?! And all the corn grew up strong and tall. And we had all the corn we could eat come fall. All we could eat.

(beat)

WIFE. *(cont.)* I liked that, when I was young and things made sense. When you planted something and it grew. Things never died before their time when I was a little girl. Never.

(beat)

Nothing I know grows like that today – strong and tall. It all seems to be some sort of invisible battle and then it just dies. Right inside of you, like some sort of under-ripe, deformed melon. And then they clean it out of you, every last piece, and pretend it never happened. It never happened. And I'm supposed to be okay with that. I'm supposed to be okay.

HUSBAND. You don't have to be okay with it? I'm not. I'm not okay with it.

WIFE. You're not?

HUSBAND. No, I'm not.

WIFE. Well, then, why are you so normal? You get up, you go to work...you move on.

HUSBAND. I haven't moved on, my love. I just get up and go to work. That's all.

WIFE. Oh, okay.

HUSBAND. Because I have to.

WIFE. Oh.

HUSBAND. If I didn't have to, I'd probably stay home all day, lie in bed and eat Bon Bons.

WIFE. Really?

HUSBAND. Well, maybe not eat Bon Bons. I'd read the
paper or something.

(WIFE *smiles*.)

You're not alone in this. I promise you that. You are
not alone.

(*pause*)

WIFE. Oh. That's good. That's really good.

(*She slowly folds the small blanket, then gets up from
where she's been lying.*)

What is it you wanted to show me?

HUSBAND. In the garden?

(*He quickly gets up.*)

WIFE. Yeah.

HUSBAND. All kinds of things. The turnips are ready to be
pulled, there's zucchini, too much zucchini, actually.
You haven't been picking it.

(*beat*)

And there're a ton of tomatoes.

WIFE. (*cautious*) Ripe?

HUSBAND. No, they're not ripe yet, but I thought if we
picked them, you know, just *before* they're ripe, maybe
then nothing would get at them...

WIFE. And they could finish ripening in the house, on the
shelf by the sink, where they're safe?

HUSBAND. Exactly.

(*waiting for her response*)

(*pause*)

WIFE. How can you still have hope? It's disgusting.

HUSBAND. I don't know.

WIFE. (*with great sorrow*) Three's too many.

HUSBAND. I know. I know. We're just going to take a look.

WIFE. We're just looking.

HUSBAND. Yes.

WIFE. Okay.

> *(leaving the blanket on the bed...)*

> Okay.

> *(They exit. Fade out.)*

End of Play

ABOUT THE AUTHOR

LISA SOLAND's other Samuel French publications include *Truth Be Told, Cabo San Lucas, Waiting* and *The Name Game.* Her work can also be found in anthologies published by Applause Books and Dramatic Publishing. From this collection, *Different, The Same Thing* and *Knots* are included in "The Best Ten-Minute Plays" anthology series by publisher Smith & Kraus. She is a member of The Dramatists Guild of America, The Alliance of Los Angeles Playwrights and the International Centre for Women Playwrights.

Ms. Soland is the founder of The All Original Playwright Workshop, where she works as Artistic Director and teacher, producing workshops throughout the United States and online.

MAN IN THE GRAY SUIT & OTHER SHORT PLAYS
Lisa Soland
Various m and f roles

From the author of *Cabo San Lucas, Waiting,* and *Truth be Told,* comes six new one act plays about love and relationship. Perfect for any theatre. Included in this book are: *The Man in the Grey Suit, Different, Red Roses, The Same Thing, Knots,* and *Come to the Garden.* All have simple casting and production requirements, all are easy to stage.

"Ms. Soland has developed several plays...all interesting, all clever, all unique. She is gorgeously talented."
– Charles Nelson Reilly (director/actor/teacher)

"*Knots?* It was the hit of the night!"
– Kenneth Kay (producer, Blowing Rock Stage Company)

"Yet another great piece from the delightful and insightful play-wright, Lisa Soland. *The Man in the Gray Suit* provides a unique look and a laugh while reminding us of the invaluable value of art in our lives.
– Gerry Athas-Vazquez (producer/writer, The Hermosa Beach Writer's Group)

"Lisa Soland's collection of six short plays is a fascinating explora-tion of how we communicate (or fail to), and an insightful exami-nation on the nature of love. *The Man in the Gray Suit* is delightfully offbeat, with - like most of her plays - an unexpected twist at the end that adds a whole new meaning to what you have just seen. Different deals perceptively with the irrationality of conflict, *Red Roses* movingly depicts the gut-wrenching moment when infidelity is revealed; *The Same Thing* is a funny and poignant play about two people who are just too alike; *Knots* looks back on a doomed college romance from the wisdom of age, and *Come to the Garden* is a sensi-tive story showing the pain of loss and the rebirth of hope. All these plays are masterfully written and stand alone individually, but have extra resonance as a collection. Highly recommended."
– Peter Colley (playwright)

"In *The Same Thing* by Lisa Soland, a man and a woman meet at a grocery store when their shopping carts collide, and discover they have almost everything in common. But will that be enough to conquer fear of commitment? Danni Wilkins and David Carter Hudson make a delightful pair."
– Tom Sime (The Dallas Morning News)

Also by
Lisa Soland...

Cabo San Lucas

The Name Game

Truth Be Told

Waiting

Please visit our website **samuelfrench.com** for complete
descriptions and licensing information

OTHER TITLES AVAILABLE FROM SAMUEL FRENCH

WAITING

Lisa Soland

Comic Drama / 6m, 6f / Unit Set

Waiting delves into the lives of twelve people who share humorous and heart-warming stories about their relationships and whether or not they waited to have sex until they were married.

"Like life, the play starts out with sex, but quickly evolves into a study of love, belonging, longing, pain, happiness and hope. Even when the characters aren't talking about their first times together, they are still waiting. Waiting for people to surprise them, waiting for a tragedy to unfold, waiting for life to begin – or end. Through all this, Soland's words bring out humor and hope, that makes life worth waiting for."
– *NoHo LA Magazine*

"*Waiting* playwright Lisa Soland starts her ostensibly light comedy with pre-marital sex and, over the course of her play, expands that theme to encompass her loss of faith in humanity in an increasingly solipsistic world. And in the journey from light to darkness…she reveals a kind of truth that transcends moral diatribe…and the play develops into a sobering indictment of our own apathy toward not only romantic relationships but the ones we forge with our fellow man as well. *Waiting* becomes a kind of strategy for getting past pre-judgments, and the play turns into a heartwarming story about restoring trust."
– *LA Weekly*

"Billed as a 'comedy about pre-marital sex,' Lisa Soland's play *Waiting* searches the passionate depths of the heart rather than keying on the fleshy surface of sex."
– *Crescenta Valley Sun*

OTHER TITLES AVAILABLE FROM SAMUEL FRENCH

CABO SAN LUCAS

Lisa Soland

Cabo San Lucas is a romantic comedy about two misfits and a postal employee who turn an apartment upside down while searching for love, courage and something to sell on Ebay. Two men break into a house and start grabbing everything they can. Little do they know that they're not alone. It seems that the owner, a young woman whose fiancé just left her, has taking a fistful of sleeping pills with some booze and is trying to sleep away her troubles for good under a blanket on the couch. When she's discovered, she's so discombobulated that it takes her a while to figure out that she's being robbed. When she does discover it, she doesn't really care (s
he was just killing herself anyway). It turns out that while the one crook is a hardened criminal, the other is just a nice guy who happened to have a gun and who has been manipulated by the other one. The nice guy is horrified when he finds out that she's trying to kill herself. The bad guy takes off with the loot, but the good one stays behind and calls 911. In the midst of Grace's attempted suicide being thwarted by two house burglars, there are many comedic opportunities. And although funny, *Cabo San Lucas* has substance and truth that will make anyone feel for our human condition and frailty.

"Those tired of playing second fiddle to the showier male roles might take a page from the author of this one act…who wrote a meaty starring role for herself…a great role for women, by a woman."
– Jenelle Riley, *Back Stage West*

"*Cabo San Lucas* also features its writer, Lisa Soland, in a lead role and Soland knows her comic strengths and plays to them. Her Grace, abandoned by her fiancé as they were about to leave for a Cabo San Lucas honeymoon (and currently being burgled by two incompetents as she attempts to bid the world good-bye with an overdose of sleeping pills), is hilarious. Her progression as the pills begin to take effect is a small tour de force of physical comedy. Jeff Charlton, as nasty burglar Jack, displays both nice timing and effective menace, and Bill Lewis, as the hapless Guy, is appealing as the boy who burgles girl, boy saves girl, boy may get girl in the end. Director Linda L. Rand paces the play well and uses her actors' abilities effectively. The show's production values are simple but perfectly appropriate for this easy-to-like afternoon."
– Janis Hashe, *NoHo La News Magazine*

OTHER TITLES AVAILABLE FROM SAMUEL FRENCH

TRUTH BE TOLD

Lisa Soland

Dramatic Comedy / 6m, 5f

"*Truth Be Told* is a full-length play that consists of eleven, one-person stories shared by a variety of personalities, all focused on getting at the truth.

"Lisa Soland's characters are quirky, heartbreaking and enchanting. In these short, expertly-tuned monologues, we understand the entire life of the characters by focusing in on events that define their lives. The characters stay with us because there are pieces of them in us all."
– Lloyd Noonan, Dramatic Writing Editor, *Quay Journal.*

"An extraordinary, well-balanced and perfect evening of theatre – so clever, so witty, so insightful and so moving.""
– Kieron Barry, *Metro Pulse.*

"Having incarnated a few of Ms. Soland's characters, I am always struck by her profoundly unique voice that somehow finds a way to touch us all. Disarmingly, her characters in *Truth Be Told* engage the audience like candy to a child, until she invites us to grow up by exposing old wounds and adding salt where we need to heal.""
– John D'Aquino, Actor/Writer.

OTHER TITLES AVAILABLE FROM SAMUEL FRENCH

THE NAME GAME

Lisa Soland

Full Length, Comedy

2m., 1f

Int.

Three misfits form a hilarious romantic triangle. Rose, a vulnerable girl who is full of life and love, is walking home late one night when she is robbed and abducted by an armed man wearing pantyhose over his head. Her shy abductor, Lincoln, is an incurable romantic who only wants to win Rose's heart. His impulsive method of courting is especially unfortunate because Rose is already engaged to Stuart, a rigidly law loving Beverly Hills police officer. Their humorous relationship and Rose's unmet emotional needs are amusingly revealed when she tells Stuart about the exciting hold up. Delighted by Lincoln's offbeat wisdom, Rose falls in love with him but finds she is pregnant with Stuart's child the handcuffs are to blame. Lincoln wants to marry Rose just the same, but she insists they seek permission from her guardian Stuart, who responds with a punch that knocks out Lincoln. At that moment Rose realizes that it is her permission that matters.

OTHER TITLES AVAILABLE FROM SAMUEL FRENCH

SAVING AMERICA & OTHER PLAYS

Ludmilla Bollow

Four short plays depicting various aspects of the American scene. These award winning productions will take you cross country– to a group on the Beach, to a selective Animal Shelter, a Firefly get-together in the woods, and a secret Government Gathering. All can be presented in one evening, or each performed separately. In these collection are:

SAVING AMERICA (*Satire / 2 m, 2 f + Voice / Bare Stage*) Strangers are brought together in mysterious gathering to "Save America", with a savage finale.

FLICKERING FIREFLIES - *(Comedy / 2 m, 2 f / Bare Stage)* Meet the Firefly Family on the night of the teens' first mating party. Magical and whimsical. For all ages.

THE BEACH CLUB - *(Comedy/Drama / 2 m, 3 f / Bare Stage)* Humor and pathos meet on the beach where an eclectic assemblage encounters the first snow of the season.

SHELTER SKELTER - *(Comedy / 2 f, 1 m or f / Minimal)* Homeless person seeks residence at the Sidney Shelton Animal Shelter. Wealthy patron, seeking a new dog, decides to adopt Annie as her pet.